~A BINGO BOOK~

New Mexico Bingo Book

COMPLETE BINGO GAME IN A BOOK

Written By Rebecca Stark

ISBN 978-0-87386-524-1

Educational Books 'n' Bingo

Printed in the U.S.A.

DIRECTIONS

INCLUDED:

List of Terms

Templates for Additional Terms and Clues

2 Clues per Term

30 Unique Bingo Cards

Markers

1. **Either cut apart the book or make copies of ALL the sheets. You might want to make an extra copy of the clue sheets to use for introduction and review. Keep the sheets in an envelope for easy reuse.**

2. Cut apart the call cards with terms and clues.

3. Pass out one bingo card per student. There are enough for a class of 30.

4. Pass out markers. You may cut apart the markers included in this book or use any other small items of your choice.

5. Decide whether or not you will require the entire card to be filled. Requiring the entire card to be filled provides a better review. However, if you have a short time to fill, you may prefer to have them do the just the border or some other format. Tell the class before you begin what is required.

6. There are 50 terms. Read the list before you begin. If there are any terms that have not been covered in class, you may want to read to the students the term and clues before you begin.

7. There is a blank space in the middle of each card. You can instruct the students to use it as a free space or you can write in answers to cover terms not included. Of course, in this case you would create your own clues. (Templates provided.)

8. Shuffle the cards and place them in a pile. Two or three clues are provided for each term. If you plan to play the game with the same group more than once, you might want to choose a different clue for each game. If not, you may choose to use more than one clue.

9. Be sure to keep the cards you have used for the present game in a separate pile. When a student calls, "Bingo," he or she will have to verify that the correct answers are on his or her card AND that the markers were placed in response to the proper questions. Pull out the cards that are on the student's card keeping them in the order they were used in the game. Read each clue as it was given and ask the student to identify the correct answer from his or her card.

10. If the student has the correct answers on the card AND has shown that they were marked in response to the *correct questions,* then that student is the winner and the game is over. If the student does not have the correct answers on the card OR he or she marked the answers in response to *the wrong questions,* then the game continues until there is a proper winner.

11. If you want to play again, reshuffle the cards and begin again.

Have fun!

TERMS INCLUDED

"A Nuevo Mexico"

Agriculture (-al)

Albuquerque

Apache

Basin and Range

Biscochito

Bolo

Border (-ed)

Camino Real

Carlsbad Cavern

Climate

Coelophysis

Francisco Vásquez de Coronado

County (-ies)

Executive Branch

Flag

Gadsden Purchase

Geronimo

Great Plains

Hot Air Balloon

Insect

Irrigation (-ed)

Judicial Branch

Lake(s)

Legislative Branch

Mexico

Mining (-ed)

Motto

Navajo

New Mexico Whiptail

Georgia O'Keeffe

Juan de Oñate

Pinyon (Piñon)

Pueblo(s)

Rio Grande

River(s)

Roadrunner

Rocky Mountains

Santa Fe

Seal

Song(s)

Squash-Blossom

Territory of New Mexico

Turquoise

Union

Vegetables

Wheeler Peak

Yucca

Zia

Additional Terms

Choose as many additional terms as you would like and write them in the squares. Repeat each as desired.
Cut out the squares and randomly distribute them to the class.
Instruct the students to place their square on the center space of their card.

Clues for Additional Terms

Write three clues for each of your additional terms.

_____ 1. 2. 3.	_____ 1. 2. 3.
_____ 1. 2. 3.	_____ 1. 2. 3.
_____ 1. 2. 3.	_____ 1. 2. 3.

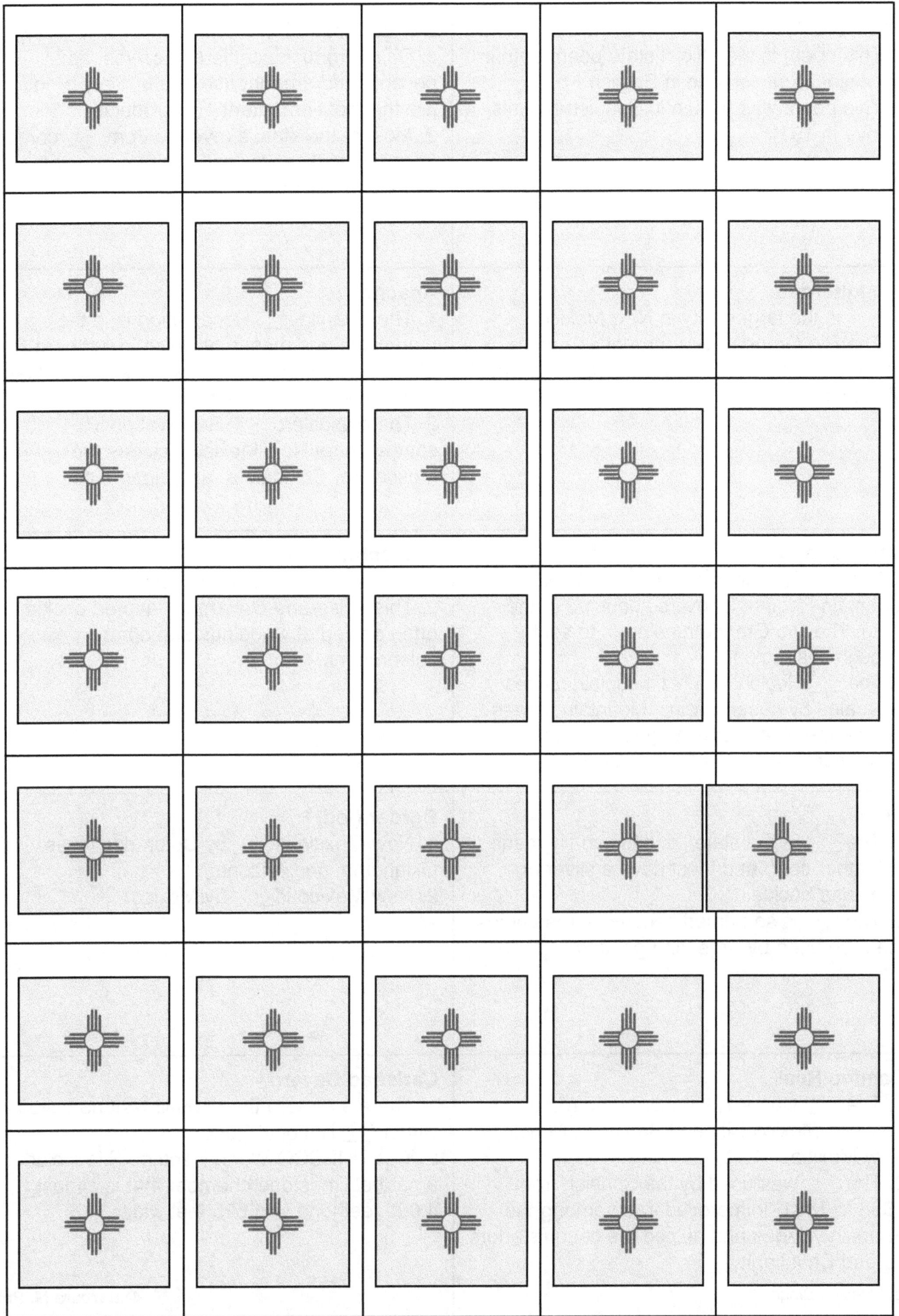

"A Nuevo Mexico" 1. This poem is the official state poem both in its original Spanish and in English. 2. This poem was written in Spanish by Luis Tafoya in 1911.	**Agriculture (-al)** 1. Dairy products, cattle and calves, hay, pecans, and greenhouse and nursery products are the most important ___ products. 2. Most of the state's revenue from ___ comes from livestock, specifically dairy products and cattle and calves.
Albuquerque 1. ___ is the largest city in New Mexico. 2. The Rio Grande flows through ___ from north to south. The Sandia Mountains are east of the city.	**Apache** 1. The Jicarilla ___ Reservation is in the mountains and mesas of Dulce in northern New Mexico. They maintain Horse Lake Mesa Game Park, an elk-hunting enclosure. 2. The Mescalero ___ Reservation in south-central New Mexico includes the Mescalero, Chiricahua, and Lipan tribes.
Basin and Range 1. The ___ Region is south of the Rocky Mountain Region. It covers about 1/3 of the state. The Rio Grande runs north to south through this region. 2. The ___ Region features mountain ranges separated by desert basins. Mountain ranges include the Guadalupe, Mogollon, Organ, Sacramento, and San Andres ranges.	**Biscochito** 1. ___ is the official state cookie. 2. This anise-and-cinnamon flavored cookie is often served at weddings and other celebrations.
Bolo 1. The ___ is the state tie. It is usually made of leather cord, and most have a silver or turquoise buckle. 2. The ___ is so named because it resembles the rope used by Argentine *gauchos*.	**Border (-ed)** 1. New Mexico is ___ by Colorado, Texas, Oklahoma, and Arizona. 2. New Mexico is ___ by Mexico.
Camino Real 1. The ___ was a 1,600-mile trade route between Mexico City and San Juan Pueblo, New Mexico. 2. The ___ was used by the Spanish from 1598 to 1881. It improved trade among the Spanish villages and helped the conquistadors spread Christianity.	**Carlsbad Cavern** 1. There are more than 100 limestone caves within ___ National Park 2. This UNESCO World Heritage Site includes a natural limestone chamber that is almost 4,000 feet long and 625 feet wide.

New Mexico Bingo

© Barbara M. Peller

Climate 1. New Mexico generally has a mild, arid or semiarid, continental ___. The ___ in the highest mountains is similar to that of the Rocky Mountains. 2. New Mexico's ___ is characterized by light precipitation totals, abundant sunshine, and low relative humidity.	**Coelophysis** 1. ___ is the state fossil. 2. Herds of this carnivorous dinosaur roamed the Southwest during the Triassic Period, about 210 million years ago.
Francisco Vásquez de Coronado 1. This Spanish explorer explored the Southwest, including what is now New Mexico. 2. ___ had hoped to conquer the mythical Seven Cities of Gold, now identified with the Zuñi pueblos of New Mexico.	**County (-ies)** 1. There were originally 9 ___. Now there are 33. 2. Bernalillo, one of the original 9 ___, is by far the largest. Albuquerque is the ___ seat.
Executive Branch 1. The ___ comprises the governor, treasurer, attorney general, auditor, secretary of state, commissioner of public lands, and public regulatory commission. 2. The governor is head of the ___ of government. The present-day governor is [fill in].	**Flag** 1. The flag of New Mexico is red and yellow. 2. A red Zia sun symbol is centered on a field of yellow on the state ___.
Gadsden Purchase 1. The ___ of 1853 sold the United States a strip of land that is now part of southwestern New Mexico and southern Arizona. 2. The ___ moved the border between the United States and Mexico to its present location.	**Geronimo** 1. Goyahkla, better known as ___, was a member of the Bedonkohe band of the Apache. 2. He fought against Mexico and the United States for their expansion into Apache tribal lands during the Apache Wars.
Great Plains 1. The the eastern third of the state is covered by the ___. There are many sheep and cattle ranches. Some dry farming and irrigated agriculture is done in the south. 2. South of the Canadian River in eastern New Mexico the ___ region is referred to as the High Plains or Staked Plains.	**Hot Air Balloon** 1. The ___ is state aircraft. 2. The Anderson-Abruzzo International Balloon Museum in Albuquerque presents the science and history of the ___.

New Mexico Bingo

Insect 1. The tarantula hawk wasp is the official state ___. 2. Two ___ are official insect symbols of New Mexico: the tarantula hawk wasp and the sandia hairstreak butterfly, the state butterfly.	**Irrigation (-ed)** 1. ___ is the act of supplying dry land with water by means of aqueducts, ditches, pipes, and other means. 2. Water is scarce in New Mexico, and most croplands must be ___.
Judicial Branch 1. The ___ interprets what our laws mean and makes decisions about the laws and those who break them. 2. The state Supreme Court is the highest court of the ___.	**Lake(s)** 1. Elephant Butte, Navajo, and Conchas are popular ___ in the state. All are reservoirs created by dams. 2. Elephant Butte Reservoir is the largest and most popular ___ in New Mexico.
Land of Enchantment 1. ___ is New Mexico's official state nickname. 2. ___ was first placed on New Mexico license plates in 1941. "Sunshine State" appeared on them before that.	**Legislative Branch** 1. The ___ of government comprises the New Mexico Senate and the New Mexico House of Representatives. 2. The ___ makes the laws.
Mexican Cession 1. The ___ 1848 refers to lands ceded to the United States by Mexico at the end of the Mexican War. 2. The United States gained some of New Mexico as a result of the ___. The rest was acquired as a result of the Gadsden Purchase a few years later.	**Mining (-ed)** 1. ___ is a very important industry in the state. 2. Petroleum and natural gas are the state's most valuable ___ products. Coal is also important.
Motto 1. *Crescit eundo* is the state ___. 2. The state ___ can be translated as "Grows as it goes."	**Navajo** 1. The ___ Nation occupies part of northeastern Arizona, southeastern Utah, and northwestern New Mexico. 2. The ___ Nation is the largest federally recognized Indian reservation in the United States by both area and population.

New Mexico Bingo

New Mexico Whiptail	Georgia O'Keeffe
1. The spadefoot toad is the state amphibian. The ___ is the state reptile. 2. This lizard is found mainly in the Rio Grande Valley. It is has a long, thin tail.	1. ___ is known for her paintings of flowers, bones, shells, stones, leaves, trees, mountains, and other natural forms. Much of her work was done in New Mexico. 2. ___ collected rocks and bones from the desert floor and made them the subjects in her works of art.
Juan de Oñate	**Pinyon (Piñon)**
1. ___ was the first colonial governor of the Province of New Mexico in New Spain. 2. In 1606 ___ was recalled to Mexico City. He was convicted of cruelty to both natives and colonists. His successor, Pedro de Peralta, founded Santa Fe as the capital of the Province of New Mexico.	1. The ___ pine is the official state tree. 2. The ___ is also called the nut pine. Its edible nuts were a staple of the Native Americans and are still widely eaten.
Pueblo(s)	**Rio Grande**
1. There are 19 ___ of New Mexico. A few are Zia, Acoma, Zuni and San Ildefonso. 2. Acoma is the oldest continuously inhabited ___ in North America. Taos ___ is the largest surviving multistoried ___ structure in the United States.	1. The ___flows through the Basin and Range Region. 2. The ___ flows through Albuquerque.
River(s)	**Roadrunner**
1. The Rio Grande, Pecos, Canadian, San Juan, and Gila are important ___ in New Mexico. 2. The Rio Grande is called an "exotic" ___ because it flows through a desert.	1. The greater ___, or chapparal bird, is the state bird. 2. This long-legged bird is a member of the cuckoo family. It walks rapidly in pursuit of prey and can run at speeds of up to 20 miles per hour or more.
Rocky Mountains	**Santa Fe**
1. The ___ extend into the central part of New Mexico from Colorado. 2. Sangre de Cristo, Nacimiento, and Jemez mountain ranges are subranges of the ___.	1. ___ is the capital of New Mexico. In 1598 Don Juan de Oñate established Santa Fé de Nuevo México as a province of New Spain. 2. The ___ Trail was a 19th-century transportation route that went from Missouri to New Mexico.

New Mexico Bingo

Seal

1. The Great ___ depicts the wings of an American eagle protectively stretching out over a smaller Mexican eagle.
2. The state motto, *"Crescit eundo,"* is on the Great ___. The year New Mexico was admitted to the Union is beneath it.

Song(s)

1. There are several official state ___.
"O Fair New Mexico" was the first.
2. The official bilingual ___ is
"New Mexico—Mi Lindo Nuevo Mexico."
The official cowboy ___ is "Under New Mexico Skies." The official ballad is "Land of Enchantment—New Mexico."

Squash-Blossom

1. The Native American ___ necklace is the official state necklace.
2. A typical ___ necklace features silver beads, called squash blossoms, with turquoise or other gem stones. Many have an inverted crescent pendant.

Territory of New Mexico

1. When it was created in 1850, the ___ included present-day New Mexico, Arizona, and parts of Colorado, Utah, and Nevada.
2. The Gadsden Purchase of 1853 fixed the southern boundary of the ___.

Turquoise

1. ___ is the state gem.
2. ___ is an opaque, blue-to-green mineral. The western and southwestern United States is the largest producer of ___ in the world.

Union

1. On January 6, 1912, New Mexico was admitted to the Union.
2. When New Mexico joined the ___, it became the 47th state.

Vegetables

1. The chile pepper is 1 of 2 state ___.
2. The *frijol,* or pinto bean, is 1 of 2 state ___.

Wheeler Peak

1. ___ is 13,161 feet above sea level. It is the highest point in New Mexico.
2. ___, the highest point in the state, is in the Sangre de Cristo Mountain range, a subrange of the Rocky Mountains.

Yucca

1. The blossom of the desert ___ plant is the state flower.
2. This flowering plant is plentiful on the plains and deserts of New Mexico; early settlers called them "our Lord's candles."

Zia

1. The ___ are an indigenous tribe of New Mexico. Like other Pueblos, they are known for their apartment-like homes made of adobe.
2. ___ are known for their pottery and use of the sun symbol. This symbol is on the state flag.

New Mexico Bingo

© Barbara M. Peller

New Mexico Bingo

Roadrunner	"A Nuevo Mexico"	Albuquerque	Geronimo	Basin and Range
Flag	Agriculture (-al)	Wheeler Peak	Navajo	Seal
Vegetables	Motto		Pueblo(s)	Yucca
Union	Santa Fe	Turquoise	Mining (-ed)	Georgia O'Keeffe
Pinyon (Piñon)	Insect	Francisco Vásquez de Coronado	Squash-Blossom	Lake(s)

New Mexico Bingo

Union	Vegetables	Judicial Branch	Rocky Mountains	Mexican Cession
Georgia O'Keeffe	County (-ies)	Border (-ed)	Santa Fe	Juan de Oñate
Carlsbad Cavern	Insect		Irrigation (-ed)	Turquoise
Rio Grande	River(s)	Motto	Zia	Basin and Range
Seal	Wheeler Peak	Francisco Vásquez de Coronado	Flag	Squash-Blossom

New Mexico Bingo: Card No. 2

New Mexico Bingo

Insect	Turquoise	County (-ies)	Mining (-ed)	Vegetables
Georgia O'Keeffe	Agriculture (-al)	Camino Real	"A Nuevo Mexico"	Hot Air Balloon
Santa Fe	Wheeler Peak		Juan de Oñate	Apache
Motto	Carlsbad Cavern	Pinyon (Piñon)	Rio Grande	Judicial Branch
Squash-Blossom	Land of Enchantment	Francisco Vásquez de Coronado	Zia	Mexican Cession

New Mexico Bingo

Motto	Juan de Oñate	Albuquerque	Land of Enchantment	Mexican Cession
New Mexico Whiptail	Bolo	"A Nuevo Mexico"	Rocky Mountains	Vegetables
Pueblo(s)	Rio Grande		Lake(s)	Geronimo
Turquoise	Agriculture (-al)	Wheeler Peak	Francisco Vásquez de Coronado	Border (-ed)
Climate	Seal	Biscochito	Squash-Blossom	Yucca

New Mexico Bingo: Card No. 4

New Mexico Bingo

Seal	Basin and Range	Santa Fe	Border (-ed)	Land of Enchantment
New Mexico Whiptail	Turquoise	Camino Real	Irrigation (-ed)	Agriculture (-al)
Albuquerque	Yucca		Navajo	Great Plains
Lake(s)	Mexican Cession	Roadrunner	Zia	Coelophysis
County (-ies)	Francisco Vásquez de Coronado	Vegetables	Motto	Pueblo(s)

New Mexico Bingo

Apache	Juan de Oñate	Judicial Branch	Mexican Cession	Yucca
Mining (-ed)	Santa Fe	Coelophysis	"A Nuevo Mexico"	Vegetables
Rocky Mountains	Climate		Bolo	Irrigation (-ed)
Francisco Vásquez de Coronado	Pinyon (Piñon)	Zia	Biscochito	Albuquerque
Georgia O'Keeffe	Border (-ed)	Roadrunner	Pueblo(s)	Executive Branch

New Mexico Bingo

Roadrunner	Juan de Oñate	Great Plains	Turquoise	County (-ies)
Georgia O'Keeffe	Mexican Cession	Insect	Agriculture (-al)	New Mexico Whiptail
Yucca	Geronimo		Irrigation (-ed)	Bolo
Motto	Rio Grande	Camino Real	Union	Carlsbad Cavern
Francisco Vásquez de Coronado	Land of Enchantment	Zia	Biscochito	Apache

New Mexico Bingo: Card No. 7

New Mexico Bingo

Pueblo(s)	Juan de Oñate	Gadsden Purchase	Mining (-ed)	Bolo
New Mexico Whiptail	Albuquerque	Rocky Mountains	Yucca	Border (-ed)
Executive Branch	Land of Enchantment		Mexican Cession	Basin and Range
Squash-Blossom	Motto	Union	Climate	Rio Grande
Wheeler Peak	Francisco Vásquez de Coronado	Biscochito	Santa Fe	Georgia O'Keeffe

New Mexico Bingo: Card No. 8

New Mexico Bingo

Irrigation (-ed)	County (-ies)	Insect	Executive Branch	Land of Enchantment
Climate	Mexican Cession	Pueblo(s)	Santa Fe	Juan de Oñate
Hot Air Balloon	Roadrunner		Agriculture (-al)	Gadsden Purchase
Coelophysis	Basin and Range	Pinyon (Piñon)	Navajo	Great Plains
Rio Grande	Zia	Camino Real	Union	Lake(s)

New Mexico Bingo: Card No. 9

New Mexico Bingo

Union	Mining (-ed)	Bolo	Rocky Mountains	Executive Branch
Yucca	Border (-ed)	"A Nuevo Mexico"	Agriculture (-al)	Mexican Cession
Land of Enchantment	Juan de Oñate		Geronimo	Carlsbad Cavern
Pinyon (Piñon)	Lake(s)	Coelophysis	Zia	Hot Air Balloon
Camino Real	Georgia O'Keeffe	Judicial Branch	Seal	Pueblo(s)

New Mexico Bingo: Card No. 10

New Mexico Bingo

Apache	Juan de Oñate	Santa Fe	Coelophysis	Georgia O'Keeffe
Gadsden Purchase	Hot Air Balloon	Navajo	Irrigation (-ed)	"A Nuevo Mexico"
New Mexico Whiptail	Mexican Cession		Judicial Branch	Insect
Camino Real	Vegetables	Zia	Land of Enchantment	Union
Climate	Francisco Vásquez de Coronado	Roadrunner	Biscochito	County (-ies)

New Mexico Bingo

County (-ies)	Basin and Range	Hot Air Balloon	Mining (-ed)	Irrigation (-ed)
Insect	Georgia O'Keeffe	Albuquerque	Biscochito	Agriculture (-al)
Roadrunner	Great Plains		Yucca	Rocky Mountains
Francisco Vásquez de Coronado	Rio Grande	Mexican Cession	Union	New Mexico Whiptail
Juan de Oñate	Gadsden Purchase	Land of Enchantment	Climate	Border (-ed)

New Mexico Bingo: Card No. 12

New Mexico Bingo

Coelophysis	Basin and Range	Apache	Hot Air Balloon	Yucca
Albuquerque	Gadsden Purchase	Mexican Cession	Irrigation (-ed)	Carlsbad Cavern
Mining (-ed)	Border (-ed)		Insect	Great Plains
Pueblo(s)	Zia	Bolo	Land of Enchantment	Union
Francisco Vásquez de Coronado	Lake(s)	Biscochito	Roadrunner	Navajo

New Mexico Bingo: Card No. 13

New Mexico Bingo

Flag	Mexican Cession	Santa Fe	Irrigation (-ed)	Climate
Border (-ed)	Roadrunner	Hot Air Balloon	Agriculture (-al)	Juan de Oñate
Coelophysis	Geronimo		Judicial Branch	Camino Real
Lake(s)	Zia	Land of Enchantment	Bolo	Apache
Francisco Vásquez de Coronado	Rocky Mountains	Carlsbad Cavern	Georgia O'Keeffe	Pueblo(s)

New Mexico Bingo: Card No. 14

New Mexico Bingo

Navajo	Irrigation (-ed)	Santa Fe	County (-ies)	Mining (-ed)
Apache	Judicial Branch	"A Nuevo Mexico"	Albuquerque	Climate
Yucca	Roadrunner		Vegetables	Juan de Oñate
Francisco Vásquez de Coronado	Hot Air Balloon	Gadsden Purchase	Zia	Coelophysis
Georgia O'Keeffe	Rio Grande	Biscochito	Executive Branch	Insect

New Mexico Bingo

Bolo	Hot Air Balloon	Gadsden Purchase	Executive Branch	River(s)
Rocky Mountains	Carlsbad Cavern	Great Plains	New Mexico Whiptail	Geronimo
Coelophysis	Basin and Range		Yucca	Insect
Motto	Border (-ed)	Francisco Vásquez de Coronado	Navajo	Union
Climate	Territory of New Mexico	Biscochito	Rio Grande	Juan de Oñate

New Mexico Bingo: Card No. 16

New Mexico Bingo

Camino Real	Song(s)	Legislative Branch	Hot Air Balloon	Flag
Navajo	Climate	Zia	Geronimo	Great Plains
Irrigation (-ed)	Pueblo(s)		Territory of New Mexico	Gadsden Purchase
Lake(s)	Georgia O'Keeffe	Union	Santa Fe	Carlsbad Cavern
Pinyon (Piñon)	Coelophysis	County (-ies)	Mining (-ed)	Basin and Range

New Mexico Bingo

Executive Branch	Land of Enchantment	Border (-ed)	Coelophysis	Rocky Mountains
Juan de Oñate	Camino Real	Pinyon (Piñon)	Yucca	Climate
Irrigation (-ed)	Carlsbad Cavern		Legislative Branch	Albuquerque
Basin and Range	"A Nuevo Mexico"	Zia	Union	Judicial Branch
Territory of New Mexico	Hot Air Balloon	Santa Fe	Song(s)(s)	Apache

New Mexico Bingo

Yucca	Apache	Hot Air Balloon	Gadsden Purchase	Union
Navajo	Mining (-ed)	Juan de Oñate	County (-ies)	Geronimo
Song(s)	Land of Enchantment		Agriculture (-al)	Vegetables
Judicial Branch	Territory of New Mexico	Pinyon (Piñon)	Rio Grande	Legislative Branch
Albuquerque	River(s)	Georgia O'Keeffe	Pueblo(s)	Biscochito

New Mexico Bingo: Card No. 19

New Mexico Bingo

Flag	Song(s)	Mining (-ed)	Hot Air Balloon	Biscochito
Border (-ed)	Insect	New Mexico Whiptail	Pinyon (Piñon)	Rocky Mountains
Basin and Range	Great Plains		Motto	"A Nuevo Mexico"
Seal	Wheeler Peak	Squash-Blossom	Rio Grande	Territory of New Mexico
Turquoise	Pueblo(s)	River(s)	Union	Legislative Branch

New Mexico Bingo

Navajo	Apache	New Mexico Whiptail	Hot Air Balloon	Seal
Basin and Range	Legislative Branch	Bolo	Gadsden Purchase	Roadrunner
Carlsbad Cavern	Georgia O'Keeffe		Song(s)	Santa Fe
Pinyon (Piñon)	County (-ies)	Territory of New Mexico	Lake(s)	Pueblo(s)
Motto	River(s)	Biscochito	Camino Real	Rio Grande

New Mexico Bingo: Card No. 21

New Mexico Bingo

Executive Branch	Judicial Branch	Legislative Branch	Albuquerque	Coelophysis
Rocky Mountains	Mining (-ed)	Vegetables	Gadsden Purchase	Agriculture (-al)
Border (-ed)	Geronimo		Roadrunner	Great Plains
Territory of New Mexico	Lake(s)	Rio Grande	"A Nuevo Mexico"	New Mexico Whiptail
River(s)	Camino Real	Song(s)	Carlsbad Cavern	Motto

New Mexico Bingo: Card No. 22

New Mexico Bingo

Bolo	Song(s)	County (-ies)	Albuquerque	Biscochito
Apache	Flag	Georgia O'Keeffe	Navajo	"A Nuevo Mexico"
Judicial Branch	Coelophysis		Squash-Blossom	Roadrunner
Carlsbad Cavern	River(s)	Territory of New Mexico	Camino Real	Rio Grande
Seal	Wheeler Peak	Pueblo(s)	Pinyon (Piñon)	Legislative Branch

New Mexico Bingo

Bolo	Pueblo(s)	Flag	Song(s)	Gadsden Purchase
Legislative Branch	Biscochito	New Mexico Whiptail	Rocky Mountains	Roadrunner
Great Plains	Executive Branch		Coelophysis	Carlsbad Cavern
Seal	Squash-Blossom	Territory of New Mexico	Camino Real	Basin and Range
Turquoise	Motto	River(s)	Mining (-ed)	Wheeler Peak

New Mexico Bingo

Motto	New Mexico Whiptail	Song(s)	Santa Fe	Legislative Branch
"A Nuevo Mexico"	Basin and Range	Navajo	Bolo	Agriculture (-al)
Lake(s)	Gadsden Purchase		Squash-Blossom	Territory of New Mexico
Vegetables	Seal	Wheeler Peak	River(s)	Geronimo
Biscochito	Flag	Border (-ed)	Climate	Turquoise

New Mexico Bingo

Legislative Branch	Song(s)	Judicial Branch	Rocky Mountains	Executive Branch
Pinyon (Piñon)	Mining (-ed)	Gadsden Purchase	Flag	Bolo
Lake(s)	Squash-Blossom		Geronimo	Motto
Camino Real	Albuquerque	Seal	River(s)	Territory of New Mexico
Great Plains	Climate	Santa Fe	Wheeler Peak	Turquoise

New Mexico Bingo: Card No. 26

New Mexico Bingo

Judicial Branch	Border (-ed)	Song(s)	Flag	Insect
Seal	Squash-Blossom	Navajo	Territory of New Mexico	Agriculture (-al)
Zia	Wheeler Peak		River(s)	Motto
Executive Branch	Apache	New Mexico Whiptail	Turquoise	"A Nuevo Mexico"
Climate	Geronimo	Legislative Branch	Vegetables	Great Plains

New Mexico Bingo: Card No. 27

New Mexico Bingo

Judicial Branch	Flag	Vegetables	Song(s)	Bolo
Insect	Legislative Branch	Squash-Blossom	Rocky Mountains	Geronimo
Wheeler Peak	Carlsbad Cavern		Great Plains	Pinyon (Piñon)
Union	Executive Branch	Georgia O'Keeffe	River(s)	Territory of New Mexico
Albuquerque	Irrigation (-ed)	Climate	Turquoise	Seal

New Mexico Bingo

Legislative Branch	Flag	Executive Branch	Navajo	Irrigation (-ed)
Rio Grande	Pinyon (Piñon)	New Mexico Whiptail	Great Plains	Vegetables
Lake(s)	Squash-Blossom		Agriculture (-al)	Song(s)
Insect	Seal	Mexican Cession	River(s)	Territory of New Mexico
Bolo	Gadsden Purchase	Turquoise	Apache	Wheeler Peak

New Mexico Bingo: Card No. 29

New Mexico Bingo

Land of Enchantment	Song(s)	Rocky Mountains	Irrigation (-ed)	Territory of New Mexico
"A Nuevo Mexico"	Flag	Judicial Branch	Geronimo	Agriculture (-al)
Lake(s)	Coelophysis		Great Plains	New Mexico Whiptail
Turquoise	Apache	Albuquerque	River(s)	Squash-Blossom
Seal	Yucca	Wheeler Peak	Legislative Branch	Vegetables

New Mexico Bingo: Card No. 30

www.ingramcontent.com/pod-product-compliance
Lightning Source LLC
LaVergne TN
LVHW061341060426
835511LV00014B/2056